How did I Begin?

by Mick Manning
and Brita Granström

W
FRANKLIN WATTS
LONDON • NEW YORK • SYDNEY

How did I begin?

You began with a special cuddle
between your mum and dad.
But after this cuddle you didn't
just pop out into the world...
their cuddle was only the beginning.
It took nine months before you
were ready to be born.

How was I made?

As they cuddled, your dad's sperms swam inside your mum and met up with one of her eggs.

What are sperms and eggs?

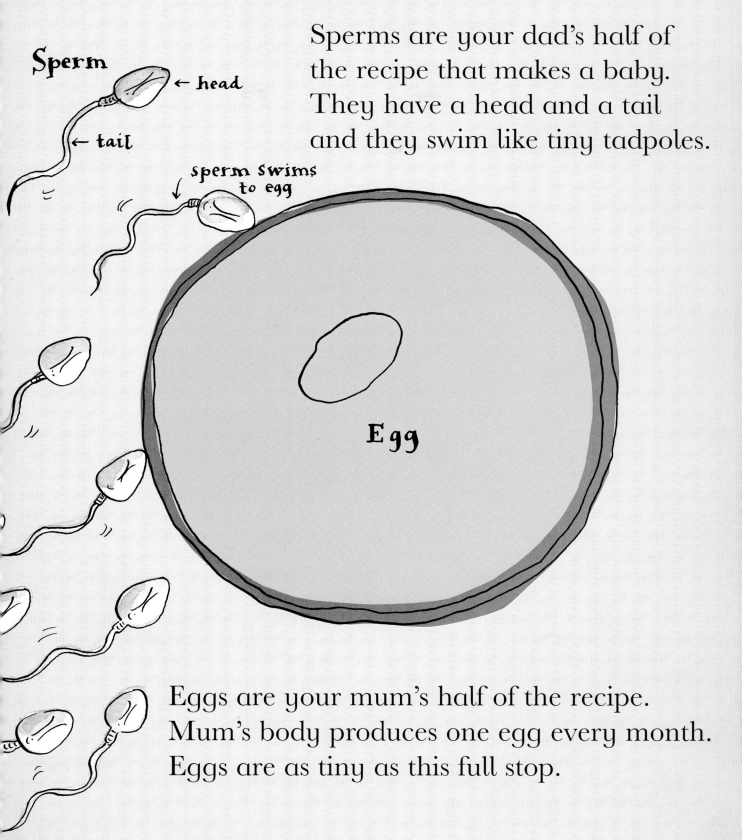

Sperm

← head

← tail

sperm swims
to egg ↓

Sperms are your dad's half of
the recipe that makes a baby.
They have a head and a tail
and they swim like tiny tadpoles.

Egg

Eggs are your mum's half of the recipe.
Mum's body produces one egg every month.
Eggs are as tiny as this full stop.

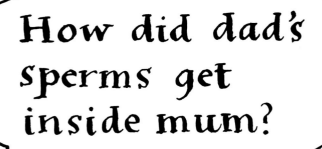

How did dad's sperms get inside mum?

As they cuddled, your dad's penis moved gently inside your mum's vagina and the sperms flowed out.

Your dad's sperms swam like crazy when they got inside your mum – they were searching for something – it was like a treasure hunt.

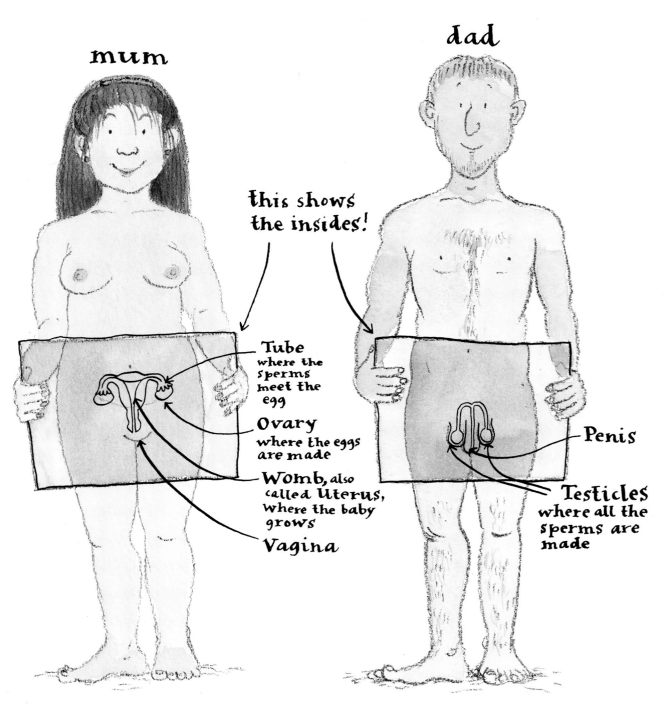

mum

dad

this shows the insides!

Tube where the sperms meet the egg

Ovary where the eggs are made

Womb, also called Uterus, where the baby grows

Vagina

Penis

Testicles where all the sperms are made

They found what they were looking for
they met mum's egg moving towards
them down a long dark tunnel!
One sperm burrowed inside the egg and
the egg made a tough skin to keep
out the other sperms.

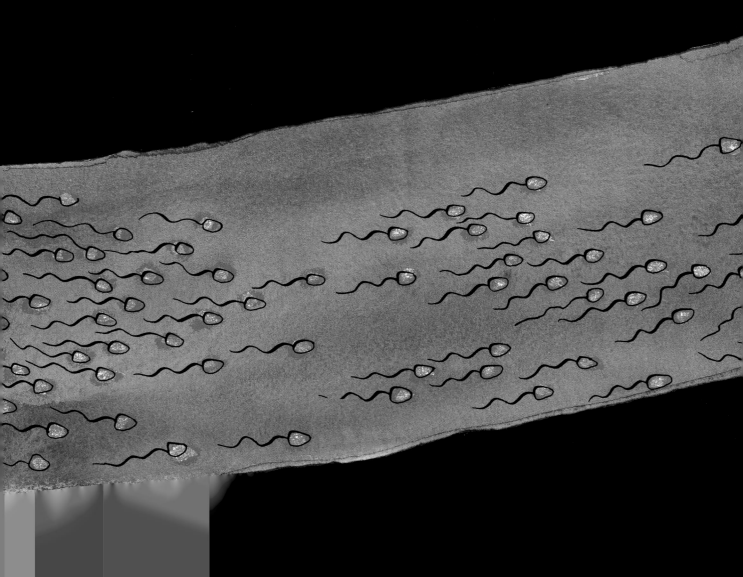

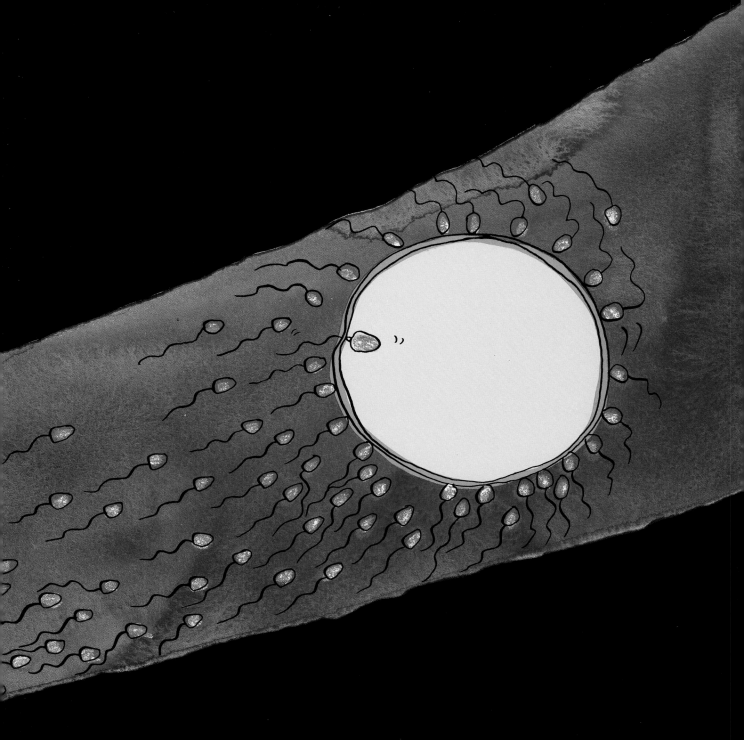

This is the split second you began!

Only one sperm out of millions wins the race to make you. That means you are a winner from the second you are made!

Together the winning sperm and your mum's egg made your first living cell.

What is a cell?

A cell is a sort of living building brick.

What makes me look like I do?

Each cell contains chromosomes which are like building instructions to make you.

You get 23 chromosomes from your mum's egg and 23 from your dad's sperm.

That's why people say, "You have got your mum's eyes" or, "You have your dad's nose."

A baby's cells have 46 chromosomes, 23 from dad and 23 from mum.

) = dad

(= mum

How do twins happen?

If two sperms find two eggs then two babies grow up next to each other!

Sometimes the first cell divides and grows into two separate babies – they are called identical twins and they look almost the same.

As you began to grow, the tiny
ball of cells that was you travelled
into a warm, dark place called
the womb and continued to grow.

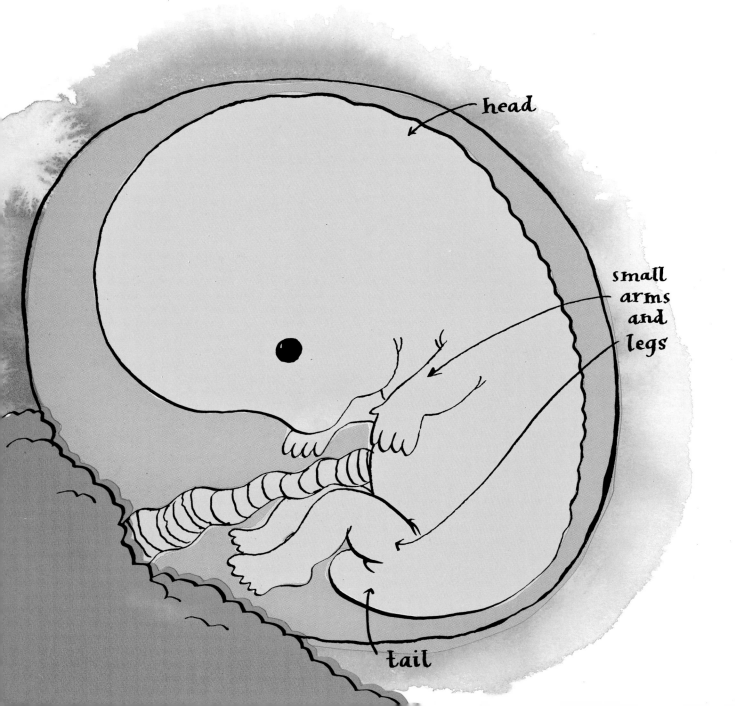

head

small
arms
and
legs

tail

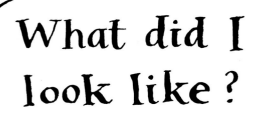

What did I look like?

After a few weeks you had a head end and a tail end. After five weeks your tiny arms and legs began to grow.

Your mum may have visited a hospital to check you were **OK**. The doctors and nurses would make sure you were well.

Perhaps a machine called an ultrasound scanner took a photo of you inside your mum.

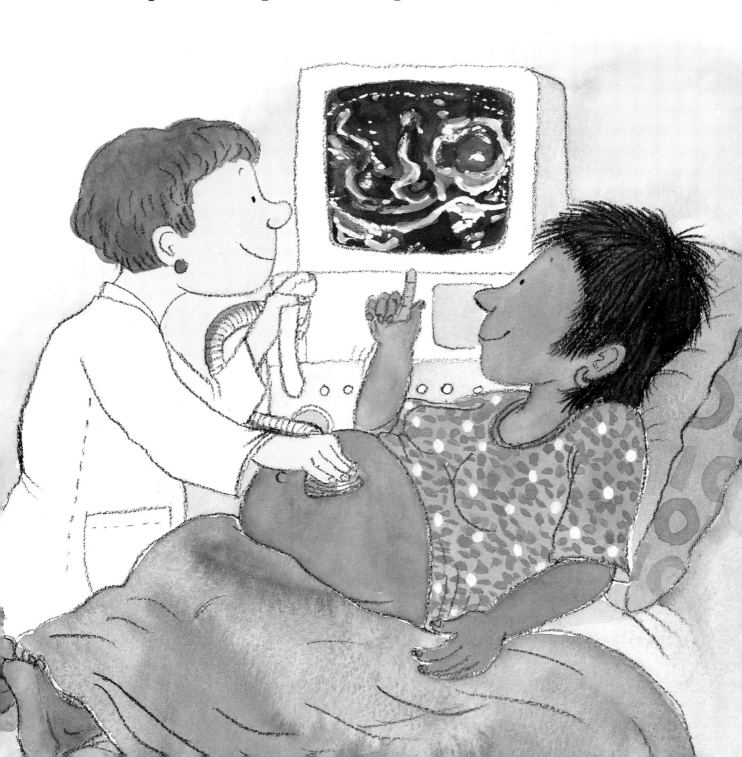

How did I breathe?

You didn't need to breathe inside your mum, all your nourishment and oxygen came in her bloodstream through a tube that joined you to her.

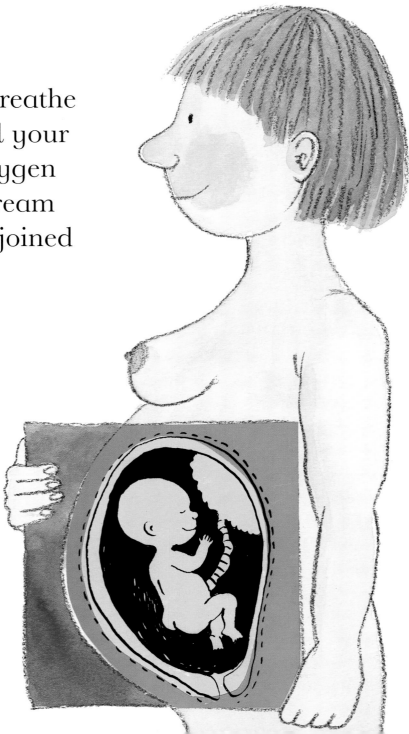

The tube is called an umbilical cord – that's where your belly button is now.

Mum's tummy stretched as you grew bigger. After five months she could feel you wriggling and kicking.

Sometimes you would play roly-poly in the middle of the night and wake your mum up!

What was it like inside mum's womb?

You floated in a bag of warm water and all around was the echo of your mum's heart like a big drum!

Could I hear things in there?

Yes you could – when mum talked you could hear her. You could listen to music as well!

Could I move about?

You could swim about. Sometimes you would drink some of the water you floated in – that would make you hiccup!

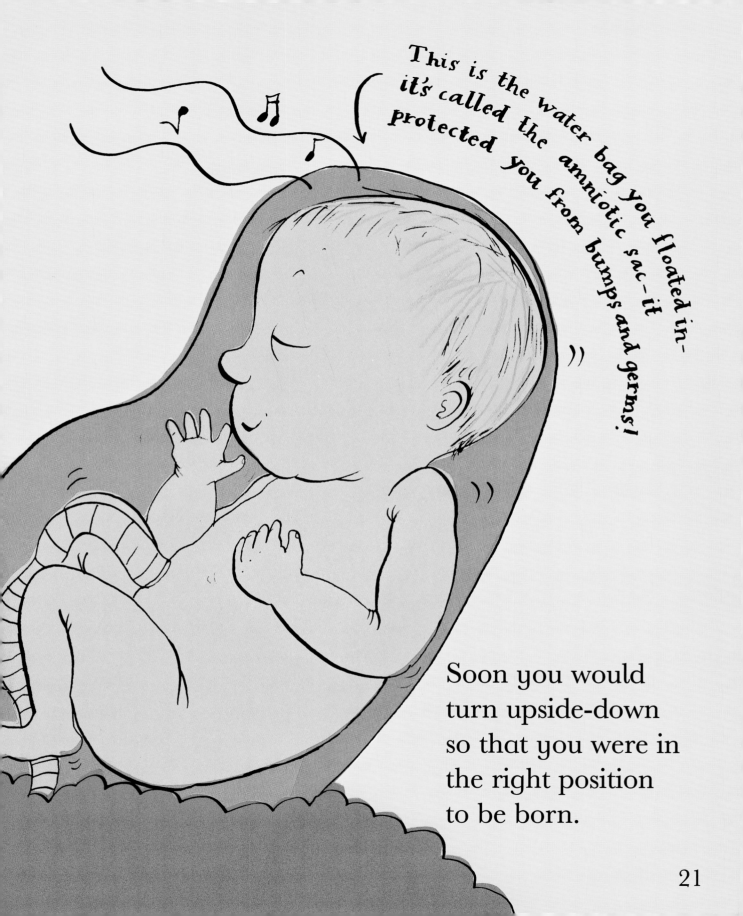

This is the water bag you floated in- it's called the amniotic sac-it protected you from bumps and germs!

Soon you would turn upside-down so that you were in the right position to be born.

21

After about nine months your mum
felt her tummy go tight, then relax.
Gradually this feeling got stronger.
This was the start of you being
born – it's called labour.

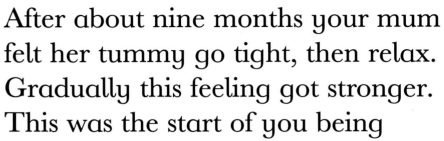

How big was
I then?

Babies can be all sorts
of sizes, but you were
probably about the size
of a rabbit!

The tight feelings your mum got in her tummy are called contractions. They can start hours before the birth will happen.

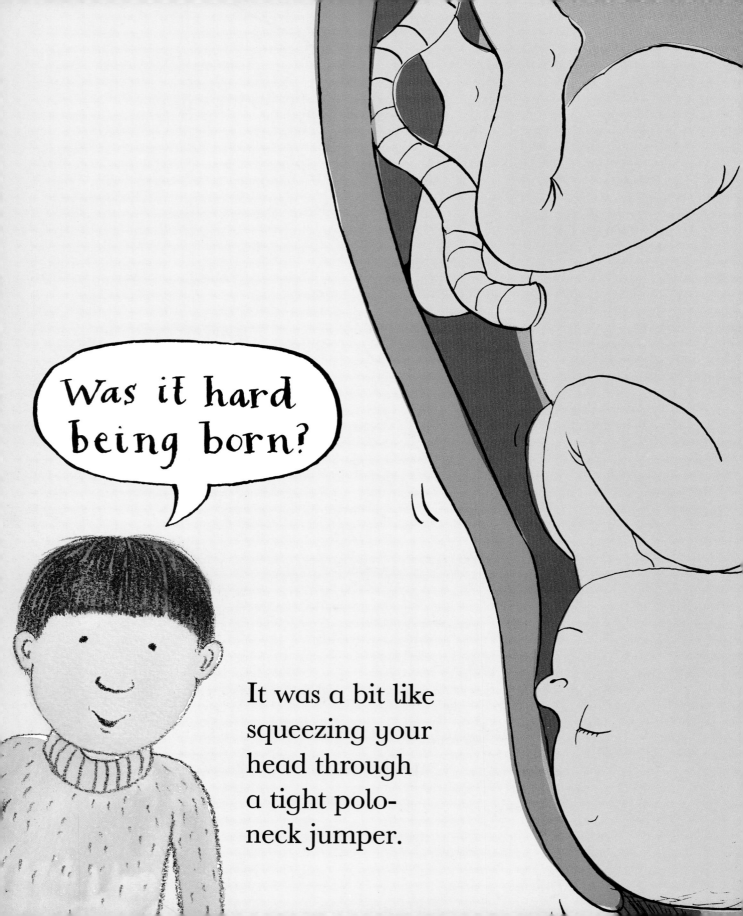

You were being squeezed out of your mum's womb. Suddenly the balloon of warm water you floated in burst! Slowly you were pushed out.

Sometimes babies can't be born like this, so a doctor puts mum to sleep and makes a small opening in her tummy and lifts the baby out — that is called a Caesarean.

First everyone looked to see
if you were a boy or a girl!
Then someone cut the umbilical
cord and weighed you.

What did I do then ?

You cried. Perhaps you wanted
to be back in that warm place,
listening to your mum's
heartbeat or perhaps you just
wanted to say hello!

So you see you started
with a cuddle between your
mum and dad. Then nine
months later there was
you, a newborn baby
sleepy in your mum's arms.

Now here you are
looking at this book!

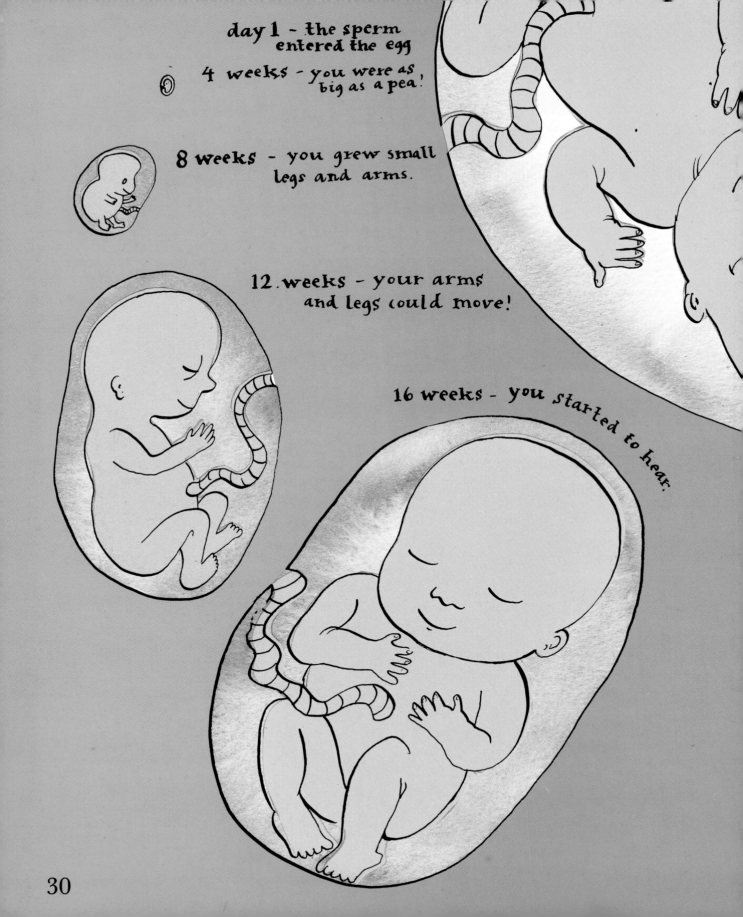

day 1 - the sperm entered the egg

4 weeks - you were as big as a pea!

8 weeks - you grew small legs and arms.

12 weeks - your arms and legs could move!

16 weeks - you started to hear.

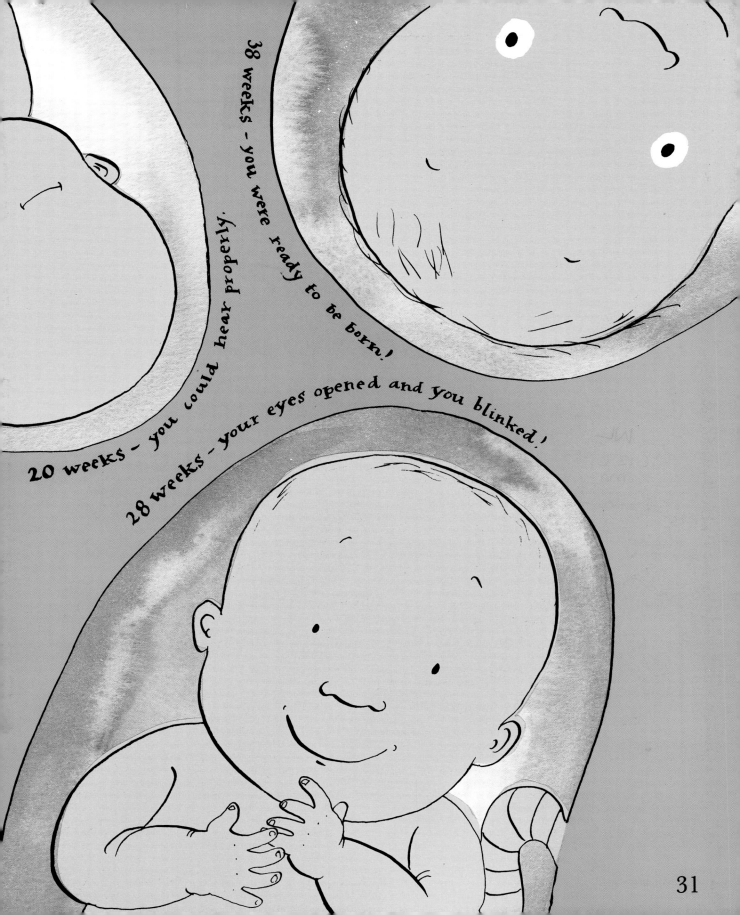

20 weeks – you could hear properly.

28 weeks – your eyes opened and you blinked.

38 weeks – you were ready to be born!

31

First published in 1997, by Franklin Watts, 96 Leonard St.,
London EC2A 4RH.

Franklin Watts Australia
14 Mars Rd
Lane Cove
NSW 2066

Text and illustrations © Mick Manning and Brita Granström 1997.
Editor: Paula Borton
Consultant: Belinda Ashon MB. BS MFFP
Printed in Singapore
A CIP catalogue record is available from the British Library.
Dewey Classification 612.6
ISBN 0 7496 2421 3

For Charlotte